The Timesheet Trap

How hourly rates are killing your consulting business

ANTHONY ENGLISH

ISBN-10: 1530691877

ISBN-13: 978-1530691876

CONTENTS

CHAPTER 1: How Much for a Camel Ride?

Supposing you're visiting some country that you've never been to before. A self-proclaimed tourist guide offers to ride you around in his buggy for a day. Or just for a couple of hours. You look at the price, and you agree it's a once-in-a-lifetime chance to experience the local culture, away from the usual tourist haunts. So you pay and off you go: getting taken to you don't know where by a tourist guide who you hopefully can trust. And it's very cheap.

Now, perhaps you can relate to this experience. It doesn't need to be a buggy ride. It could be a camel ride or whitewater rafting. The point is *you don't really care where you go*, as long as you have a good experience and you get back safely. And the trip is charged by the hour.

Pilot by the Hour

Now, compare that with a different travel experience. You want to charter a flight which is going to take you to Booradulla - a remote location for your business. Let's say it's a six-hour flight.

What's important to you? How long it takes? How much per hour? Supposing the pilot tells you: "here are my hourly rates" and then says it's going to be about six hours. Would you agree to pay for the flight *after* the pilot hands you his timesheets?

And what happens if the flight takes longer than estimated? Would the pilot warn you about 5 and a half hours into the flight that it's going to take longer than expected? I can just see that conversation:

"I'm afraid due to unforeseen circumstances, we're going to miss our ETA by two hours. You can either agree to pay me the extra two hours, or here's a parachute."

The Crazy Pilot

You can already see that that pilot must be crazy for wanting to hand you a parachute and hit the eject button. But the pilot would also be mad for agreeing to sign up to a timesheet-driven, pay-by-the-hour charter flight that he only gets paid for after bickering over how long the flight took.

Yes, the pilot should have given you a better estimate of how long the flight would take, but sometimes delays happen. So, perhaps you're thinking the pilot should have factored that into his hourly rate.

Now, what if the pilot knew a way of shortening the flight? What if he used his flying experience, knowledge of tail winds and how to get to Booradulla without taking the slow path? Supposing the pilot can land you safely in, say, four hours? At an hourly rate, he actually gets penalized for his ability to get you there faster.

"Just Get Me There!"

So maybe the passenger and the pilot could come up with a totally different plan that looks something like this:

"Here's the flight to Booradulla. I'm *estimating* it's going to take about six hours. However, there are a lot of things that are out of my control. It may take us over six hours. But, then again, I could use my expertise and land you there well ahead of the estimated time. That would get you to the Booradulla Hotel faster so you can get more time to settle in or get on with your business. So here's the price. You pay for the ticket up front and getting you there safely is my problem. Deal?"

I'm guessing you're going to say: "Take my money. Forget about timesheets. Just get me there!"

The Timesheet Trap

This book is my attempt to talk you out of flying by the hour, and to talk you into charging for the result. It's aimed primarily at Information Technology consultants, because that's what I know best. But I think the principles I draw on here are applicable across other industries and are going to be helpful for all kinds of consulting work.

So my aim is to sow at least some seed of doubt in your mind about whether charging by the hour is smart for your business. Let me tell you at the outset that I have been charging by the hour for seven years, and I'm in an industry and in a country where hourly rates – or at least daily rates – are almost universal. But I'm moving away from that model, charging sometimes four times more than my hourly rate and *my clients love it!*

No more timesheets! No more getting paid sometimes weeks after the work is completed. And no more of clients – or myself – wondering "what did we achieve by paying all those hours?"

I must say that for me as a consultant, not having to complete timesheets has been a huge relief. If you're working on site or dedicated full-time to a particular project, it's not so hard. But if – like me – you aim to provide high value work in a very short time, then timesheets simply impede that productivity. You're wondering: "do I charge for this meeting? What about these emails that I've been copied on and that I don't really have to answer? Or the ones where I *do* provide a short answer, that can really remove a project roadblock."

The Fine Print

Let me also say right now that this book is not going to walk you through *how* to stop using hourly billing. That may be a disappointment to you, but there's a method to my madness.

You see, I've had this conversation with probably dozens of consultants just like you. I've also spoken to a few of my clients. And what I find, almost universally, is that the transition from hourly billing and timesheets is not a difficulty with the mechanics. It's more a psychological one in the mind of the consultant. In fact, I'd say that this is my number one aim – and mainly my only aim – of this book, to pull you out of what I call the Timesheet Trap.

What about the clients?

And if you're an end client who hates the notion of timesheets (or some other time tracking methodology), and who loves the idea of paying for a result, based on a predictable price, then I'm hoping this book will also have a lot of "aha" moments for you. Maybe it's something you could share with colleagues or consultants, who might at least like to consider charging you for a safe flight to Booradulla, not for a pilot who charges by the hour.

But it is written primarily for the consultants who find themselves in the Timesheet Trap.

CHAPTER 2: The Specialist Consultant

Let's assume you've got a great niche. You solve expensive problems for businesses that are willing to pay to have those problems to be solved.

So, you've cornered your market – either by industry or geography or technology or some other angle that makes you stand out.

Good for you!

You have a successful consultancy and you charge yourself out at X per hour.

Now, here are three reasons (off the top of my head) that you are doing damage to your business by charging by the hour:

Reason #1 You are breaking down trust with your client

Reason #2 You are leaving money on the table (lots of it!)

Reason #3 You are setting yourself up for resentment because of reasons #1 and #2.

Frankly, you're killing your relationship with your client,

and if that isn't enough to scare you, then you should stop reading.

How could I possibly change from hourly billing?

I know, I know. You're probably thinking:

"Who is this guy? He doesn't understand my market."

"Hourly billing is the standard across the industry. I can't change it."

So, first things first. Who am *I* to be telling you *not* to bill by the hour? And even if I can show you that moving away from hourly billing is going to be great for your business, how on earth are you going to implement such a massive change of mindset?

If you want to change from hourly billing (because it's *BAD* **TM**), the first (and maybe only) person you have to convince is yourself. You see, you probably don't have any reason to bill by the hour other than "everybody does it." Now, if I show you that not everyone *should* charge out hourly, then I'll have to show you three things:

1. Why hourly billing is bad for your business
2. Why it's bad for your clients; and

3. What you can do to change the culture.

Full disclaimer: part 3 on how to change the culture will not be a step-by-step guide to moving away from hourly billing. The focus of this book will be for you as a consultant – or possibly as an end client – to see how billing by the hour can damage the consultant/client relationship, because it's bad for both parties.

Controlling the Sales Process

I have to say that changing anything to do with how you price depends on you having a substantial control over the sales and pricing process. So, if you're an independent consultant who deals directly with companies, *and* if the people in those companies you deal with have some decision-making ability, or directly control the budgets, then this book is for you.

And if none of that is true, then it's probably still worth your while to understand why hourly rates can kill a consulting business. For that matter, if you're on the other side of the desk, and you *are* that client who is currently paying consultants at hourly rates, then you will probably get some unique perspectives on what happens behind the scenes when consultants or agencies propose an hourly rate or estimate how long a project will take to complete.

But first, let me tell you a little of my own recent history as a consultant.

My Consultancy Life In 200 words

In 2007 I moved from being a full-time employee at an Information Technology company in Sydney to being a contractor. I was driven by the attractive rates of a contractor, which on a per-hour basis were upwards of 50% higher than being an employee.

As a father of a young and growing family (we had five children at the time and have had two more since then), it was hard to resist the lure of contracting rates that *on the face of it* seemed much higher than a full-timer's salary.

My first contract for six months was extended twice, until I left for another similar contract, both in the financial industry. My field of expertise is IBM Power Systems – the midrange computers that are still pretty widely used for high-end companies running Oracle, SAP and several other prominent applications and databases.

Moving Into Freelancing

For a few years I would accept the going rate for my contract, which was either an hourly rate or – in some cases – a day rate. That was almost always channeled through an agency – primarily because the big companies I was working with didn't typically want to work with a solopreneur.

But I moved into freelancing (as I then called it – I wouldn't use that term about myself now). And I started getting known with much smaller companies doing much smaller bits and pieces of work – sometimes as little as two hours of work.

"That all sounds pretty standard: hourly or daily rates."

Yes. Quite right. And I found it frustrating. Apart from the long-term six month contracts, I didn't have any regular income, so it was a question of waiting for a call – usually from a small IBM Business Partner who needed my skills to set up a system for their clients.

Look at the model here: the client of the business partner would contact that BP, and they would get in touch with me. I would often launch into a project or an emergency fix at my hourly rate. The BPs – with whom I have always had a good relationship – would put their cut above whatever I was charging them. And I didn't bill up front, because you had to put in time sheets and then invoice based on the chargeable hours.

So, I had the up front work, keeping a record on time sheets (or whatever system the business partner used for time tracking – usually very basic Excel spreadsheets). I'd send the time sheet to the BP, along with the invoice, and then hope to get paid a couple of weeks later. Some BPs were really good payers. Some were not. They never got penalized by me for paying me late … other than an annoying email or two.

Project By The Hour

Typically, the project – such as an installation of an IBM Power System or an upgrade – or maybe a data centre migration – would run for a few weeks, but it would be extremely rare for me to be on that full-time.

I would be an on-call resource (another term that people use about me, but I don't use it about myself). I was a commodity (ditto) who would be like a one-man cloud service.

This created a great dilemma for me. Generally – by which I mean always – there are emails to answer around a project, or after the project, which are not really included in the cost of the project. Being guilt-ridden about charging for emails that only took me a few minutes to answer, I wouldn't charge. If I was writing a script (think of a computer program), or actually changing something when I was working from home, I might bill for that in half-hour slots.

The Hourly Discount

I have to say that I rarely if ever was able to raise my prices, even though my skills were growing all the time. The increased skill level meant I could achieve much more quickly what might take others four times as long. That was usually because there's a lot of what I'd call cross-fertilisation when you're working on a number of different projects for different companies throughout the year.

You may spend two days troubleshooting some performance problem at Company A, and then take the fix that you learn from that when you're at Company B. That two-day experience at Company A means that you can resolve Company B's similar performance problem in 10 minutes … or maybe even prevent the performance problem from ever occurring in the first place.

By now you must be starting to see that hourly billing was working against me. The faster I worked (which was good for the client), the less I earnt (bad for my business).

A Script in Time

Now, it seemed to me that I had what we might call a big, expensive problem. I was getting paid for the hours I worked, not for my knowledge or my ability to make projects run much smoother and faster. For example, if I was working on a project with, say, 25 other people on a weekend, and they were waiting for me to do my bit before they could get on to their respective tasks, then if I could shortcut my part by, say, two hours, I was saving 25 people two hours of waiting.

At the beginning of a weekend, that may be no big deal, but believe me, when you've got your bank or large retailer's mission-critical system hanging off on a successful project, and the system has to be back up again by Sunday night, that two hour saving becomes very, very valuable. If a change of some kind has to be rolled back, the whole change has to be rescheduled, so even if none of the 25 people are getting paid for their weekend work, without that script or system tweak that shaved two hours off the weekend, the big change could have a much bigger impact on a lot of people – even if there is no system outage.

I'm no hero

I don't mean to present myself as a hero or a guru. I could relate similar examples of massively significant time-saving achievements from Subject Matter Experts in fields I know nothing about.

What I'm trying to show is that the hours you put into a technical problem are not necessarily reflective of the value to the business. In fact, a small contribution (in terms of time) could have a massive benefit to the business. Which is not reflected when you bill by the hour.

The Big Epiphany

Now, by this stage I hope I have at least sown a small seed of doubt about the value of billing by the hour.

So now, let me justify my earlier claims that billing by the hour can be damaging for your business.

Here, once again, are three reasons that I gave to show you why hourly billing is bad for your business. In fact, I'll add that it's *bad for business*, including your client's business. First, let's get into the claims I made at the start of this book.

CHAPTER 3: Why Hourly Billing is BAD

Billing by the hour is so entrenched, especially in the IT industry, that it seems absurd even to question it. So, what's wrong with billing by the hour, completing timesheets of what you've done (or using some time tracking software) and then sending the invoice off?

There are *plenty* of reasons why that model is fundamentally flawed, but let me give you three:

Reason #1 You are breaking down trust with your client

Reason #2 You are leaving money on the table (lots of it!)

Reason #3 You are setting yourself up for resentment because of reasons #1 and #2.

Reason #1: Breaking Down Trust

Hourly billing breaks down trust between the client and

the consultant. Why? Because it effectively postpones the decision of how much a project is going to cost.

Here's how the hourly-billing dance usually goes (and it's all about stepping on each others' toes)

Client: "What's your hourly rate?"

Consultant: "About $X per hour."

Client: "That's a little above our budget."

Consultant: "Alright. I can do it for 15% off that. Let's call it $Y."

Client: "And how much time do you think this project will take?"

Consultant: "Oh, it's hard to say, but as an estimate let's call it 100 hours."

The client hears "100 hours" at $Y. Total budget.

"Let's add some fat"

Already that 100 hours estimate is a complete ballpark figure. The consultant is thinking this project might take something less than that, but they've added in some "fat". (This is the term used in the industry, to make up for the fact that we're pretty rotten at estimating how long a project takes. And it's rare that we over-estimate!)

The story so far

The consultant then begins the work, and starts sending time sheets, which the client is meant to peruse and approve. After the approval, the invoice is paid.

Now, that's a massive oversimplification of the process. The consultant's time sheets may not always be an accurate reflection of what they've really spent their time on. The reason is that time sheets to a consultant are a necessary evil, and are often (unfortunately) only completed a few days after the work has been done, just in time for the time sheet approval cut off time. That means that the client has to assume that the time sheets are accurate, and even the most honest and ethical consultant has an at least unmentioned motive to have the time sheets filled in to look good to a client.

Timesheets don't work in the client's interest. They are purely for the justification of the consultant's billing time, so the very existence of them makes for a potential source of conflict of interest.

Building Business Trust

When you have any business relationship, if you want it to work well, it has to be mutually beneficial. For a client / consultant business relationship, that usually means the money has to be valuable to both. By that, I mean that the client is making an investment – for example, on building a new website – and there must be a good return on that investment: the ROI. There might be a myriad of ways that the client will value that website. It could be for prestige, or to get more sales online, or simply to please someone else in the business. But there will be *some* value to the client.

Now, the consultant, too, needs to be rewarded for his contribution to the project. That will usually be in terms of money, although there may be other, less tangible, gains that he has in mind. For example, he may be looking for a strong brand name to have on his profile of happy clients. Or he might be looking for testimonials from people whose opinion is valued.

Whatever the non-financial reward, let's make it simple and just put it down to how much the consultant gets paid.

Right now, we can see a conflict: the client pays (which is a loss for the client) and the consultant gets paid (a gain for the consultant). Now the client is naturally inclined to lower that rate while the consultant is wanting to increase it. So they come up with an agreed rate: this is basic negotiation over benefits, risks and so on.

The Notion of Competition

We usually think of competition as us vs. them. One wins, the other loses. And the hourly rate instance – with an estimate of hours – is a perfect example of this to and fro between the client and the consultant, until they agree on a rate. In reality, this is usually a very quick conversation, and doesn't generally involve the back and forth that might be involved in other transactions, such as buying a house.

But I'd like to invite you to think of competition in a very different light. And this will be a significant piece in the puzzle as we move away from hourly billing, with an arrangement that builds trust, rather than undermines it.

The etymology of the word "competition" is the Latin *cum* +*petere.* The word *petere* means "to strive for", and the prefix "cum" means "together". So the word competition might be understood as to strive together.

Striving Together

So, working towards a goal – together. That's a whole new way of thinking of competition, isn't it? Could that work in business?

The short answer is: not if the two parties are fighting against each other.

How else does hourly billing break down trust? Well, look at what happens when the project gets underway and then gets close to its projected estimate. Suppose we get close to the 100 hours. The consultant has to come back to the client with a warning: "we're using up the hours." And the client might say: "but you told me it was going to be 100 hours." Then the consultant says: "well, that was an *estimate*." Then there's a "discussion" on what is, or isn't in scope, what the deliverables were, and then the negotiation *really* begins. That will end either with the consultant getting paid for more hours, or the consultant not getting paid for more hours (but having to do them anyway), or some other compromise. The client may be disgruntled and put the project on hold, or even look for some other consultant who will be able to rescue the project.

All in all, it's a big mess, unless that original estimate was accurate (which is rarely the case).

In fact, if the project has blown out its estimated time, then if the consultant isn't getting paid for the extra time, he'll look to recuperate costs some other way. There is a continual lingering question about every hour: "is this chargeable?" To tell you the truth, I seriously thought about calling this book "Is this chargeable work?"

Reason #2 Against Hourly Pricing: Leaving Money on the Table

Clearly, the consultant ought to get paid what he is worth. And if he undercharges his hourly rate – which very, very often happens – the consultant *doesn't* get paid what he is worth. So what is the consultant worth?

Short answer: more.

Long answer: lots more.

But you as a consultant need to convince the client of that. And if you don't do that, then the client may – with all good will – pay less than you're worth, because you didn't think to charge any more.

And why didn't you think to charge more? Hint: it's because you relied on an hourly rate, which may be based roughly on market rates. True, you didn't actually make the hourly rate up, and the estimate is probably way too low (even including "a little bit of fat"). So, all in all, we've got a situation where the hourly rate is too low, the estimate is a guess, and the client is happy enough … until the estimated hours start to get used up.

This is clearly not a good situation for the consultant. And, while on the surface, it seems better for the client, in practice it creates a situation of continuous tension. You don't want the client wondering: "am I getting charged for this?" It pays to have a long-term client who is convinced that you're working to help that client with their business problems. Hourly pricing doesn't always achieve that. In fact, it's a bit like going to a restaurant and choosing based on price alone. What if you could have a prepaid offering, that covers all the meals you're going to eat, and then you could choose based on the best meal for you, rather than the chef's hourly rate and how long it will take to cook?

Reason #3 Against Hourly Rates: Resentment

From what we've seen so far, it's clear that the ultimate result of an hourly rate arrangement is that the consultant may well feel that he's giving great value that isn't recognized properly. Even if it's a relatively high hourly rate, the experienced consultant can deliver the result more quickly and safely than a less expensive and less experienced consultant. So the senior one gets penalized for working faster.

For the honest consultant, this situation is likely to lead to resignation ("it is what it is, I just have to put up with it"), or resentment. There's a high chance that senior consultant will come to look for greener pastures. The reason is that the consultant has agreed to an hourly rate that is well below the value that he perceives the client ought to be paying. True, that was the original agreement and a deal is a deal. So the consultant will be resentful, or simply put up with what he knows is an inadequate arrangement.

Attempts to Tweak the Hourly Charging Model

Now, if you're thinking "more fool the consultant for agreeing to a lower rate than he's worth", then you're following my argument very well.

You see, the hourly rate – and a low hourly rate at that – doesn't have to be the *de facto* arrangement.

Complicating the Example

In the example I've given, I've had a single consultant dealing with a single person "the client" about an agreed hourly rate for an estimated project timeline.

In practice, there are many more ways this arrangement is

likely to be more complex.

Number one among these is an intermediary agency: a middle man. The agency is finding the project and marrying up the client with a suitable consultant. The agency are doing the negotiations with the client and with the consultant, and taking a handsome cut along the way. The longer the project goes on, the more commission the agency gets. That is the arrangement, and the client pays, even though the consultant doesn't see the reward.

Added to this is the fact that the agency is often expecting a minimum number of hours worked. So if the consultant is perhaps wary of charging for hours where he is not working as expected – for example, if he's late for work, or has a long lunch (even with the clients' colleagues) – the consultant may still be expected to put in a time sheet for the full weekly hours.

The Convenient Timesheet

In any financial contract there has to be a common currency, a measure by which both parties agree that this is a fair deal. Now, surprisingly, that measure isn't money. At least, it's not *only* money. If we suppose a simple exchange: "you sell me three cows and I will give you this much money", then the money exchange is only one way.

Now an hourly rate agreement says: "I will give you this much *time* and you will pay me this much per hour." This kind of agreement doesn't account for the value of the time, or the fact that the consultant, as an example, is able to generate much more value to the end client in some circumstances than others. The consultant is being paid to keep a seat warm.

All of that is very convenient, because we can say: "this many hours, and here's my timesheet." Hours worked = hours charged (except for the unchargeable hours!). And that makes the hours the point of agreement – or disagreement – between the consultant and the client.

No Accounting for Trust

You could be forgiven for thinking that this kind of to-and-fro perusing of timesheets is not a normal arrangement, and that if it comes to that, the relationship between the two parties has broken down, or is breaking down.

For that matter, if the consultant is too lazy to be working well, it sounds like the client may be working with the wrong consultant. After all, the client should be able to trust the consultant, so that the hours worked are really a reflection of the valuable time that the consultant has put into the client's project.

My answer to that is yes, it's true that the client should be able to expect good work from the consultant, but that isn't going to be measured in terms of hours. What's more, the requirement to put it in hours only serves as an attendance rollcall, also known as a timesheet. ☺

Charging for Creativity

I remember many years ago I was working for a non-profit that wanted to get a new logo. This was long before the days of the internet where you could organize this sort of thing online or even design your own with some fancy tools, so they went to a printing and graphic design company, if I remember rightly.

I remember the boss asking this graphic designer what we'd be getting for the amount quoted to design a logo. The graphic designer started his answer with something like: "half an hour of someone staring at a blank wall." Now that answer truly shocked me, because I thought it was unprofessional and – to tell you the truth – a very expensive half hour of wall-staring for the end client.

However, today I can see that the graphic designer was onto something. We were paying for creativity, not for how long he would spend "staring at a blank wall." And in the end, the logo turned out to be a very effective way of sharing the non-profit's ideals with its members and supporters. It was a big changer of the mood of the members (perhaps you'd call it branding these days) and was a sign that other things were happening in the non-profit. And the difference was paying for creativity, rather than paying by the hour.

Tweaking the Hourly Rate Model

There are some companies and countries where a day rate is used instead of an hourly rate. In some ways, this is a more equitable arrangement, as it allows for the give and take of time that happens due to lunch breaks, lighter work loads and so on. It also allows the client to have more predictability about the costs of consultants: a day will be a day, even if the consultant ends up working a little extra … or a lot.

So the day rate still returns us to the same problem of conflict between consultant and client. Some clients are happy to be very flexible, but others are more rigid, so that a day consists of a minimum of , say, 7.5 or 8 hours, but if the consultant works longer – even two, three or more hours (as may well happen in IT, for example) – the consultant is effectively working for free for those hours. In principle, the consultant should factor that in when agreeing to a day rate but in practice, the day rate is unlikely to be sufficient to cover the amount of free time that is being worked.

Downtime and Hourly Rates

Back to the problem of hourly rates and the quandary it can put the consultant in. Supposing you are a consultant working at the client's office. Then, clearly, you charge by the hour. Now maybe you're working remotely. Once again, you could charge for the time when you're focused on that client. You may carve out half a day, or half an hour, and that goes on the time sheet.

But since your day can be charged out by the hour, or part thereof (maybe even in 15 minute increments), the temptation is to take on another project for a different company – especially when the first project slows down, such as when you're waiting for new information or for others to get back to you.

Now, supposing you're focused on the project for Company B, or maybe doing something else with your time (not necessarily chargeable work at all), and then you get a phone call from Company A. It could be a short call, perhaps a request for something small. Do you charge or not?

What about if you have to answer an email? Just a short one, that might take you a few minutes. Give and take, right? But then a couple of hours later, there's a reply that you need to give. Or again, supposing you get an email that you're *not* required to answer. You still need to read it and give it your attention, *in case* you need to take some sort of action. Do you charge for this? Yes or no?

Perhaps you think this is being scrupulous. Maybe you're thinking "I should just charge for whatever time I'm thinking about the client's project." Or else you'll show clemency: unless I log into the client's system or am actively doing some documentation for their project, I won't charge.

The point is that you, the consultant, are in a quandary, and you'll either have to give rock-solid justification for the time you've spent answering (or not answering) emails, or else you'll have to be aware of the client's needs, be ready to share your expertise, but not charge them until you're actually in a position where you have to respond.

Messy, isn't it?

One way that this is "resolved" is by the client insisting you be on site, or at least on a conference call, because [to put it bluntly] they might not be able to trust you.

CHAPTER 4: Hourly Billing: Is there a better way?

I was recently on a conference call with consultants from three other countries, and all of them were discussing the challenges of hourly billing and timesheets: to bill, or not to bill, that is the question. I was struck by how much these consultants had to justify to themselves whether or not they charged for emails, travelling time etc. It occurred to me that maybe the clients weren't going to be too worried about micromanaging these hours, but the consultants felt that they ought to do it anyway.

This conference call made me realize just how forced it was to impose a timesheet regime on consultants who ought to be getting paid for their knowledge, not their physical or online presence.

Then I saw that this was exactly the problem: the consultants were getting paid for their time, not their value.

I realize that the notion of "value" is a pretty elusive one. So we resort to market rates. And where do those market rates come from? Whatever is currently paid in similar industries or businesses for similar skills.

The answer to that is: yeah, right. How can you compare? Take a simple example – not directly from the world of services, but it's perfectly applicable.

How much does a meal cost?

Of course, your answer will be: "that depends." It depends on a lot of factors, such as the location of the meal (is it in a classy restaurant, or is it cooked at home?) And ingredients. And the experience of the chef. And the time of day (breakfast is rarely more expensive than the evening meal, for example). And many other factors.

So, how much does a meal cost? Do you add up the cost of the chef, plus the cost of the ingredients, and the rent of the restaurant and so on? Add them all together and divide them by the number of meals you'll sell in a year, add a little bit of profit ("add a little bit of fat") and bingo! You've got the price of the meal!

That's not at all how the prices of meals are calculated. At least, you can't compare an expensive meal with a cheaper one in a budget restaurant and explain it all by rent, ingredients and the hourly rate of the chef.

No, people have all kinds of reasons to pay for a meal, and those reasons may be only very superficially related to the cost of making it.

The most important point in pricing a meal as well as pricing a service is not how much it costs you. It's how much the client values it.

High Value Doesn't Mean A Low Price

So, you may be ready to pay a lot more for a meal because of the atmosphere of the restaurant, or because of the reputation of the chef, or the timing of the meal. For example, if you want to eat a meal at a super popular restaurant on New Year's Eve overlooking Sydney Harbour with the fireworks, that meal is worth much more to you than exactly the same meal in the same restaurant on a cold and stormy day in the middle of winter.

How do you find the price of the meal? You don't ask the neighbouring food places. They may sell cheap hamburgers, but still the luxury restaurant has clientele.

How do you find the price of the meal? You ask the clients! And even odder than this – the clients won't (on the whole) choose the meal based on the price. Or – more accurately – the high price isn't stopping them buying the meal. In fact, the high price may make them think the meal is worth as much as it is priced. It's expensive, so it must be good!

Now, I know you must be thinking: there's a natural limit for the price of a meal. And you can't just charge whatever you want. No, definitely not. The natural limit should be the reasonable value of the meal to the restaurant patron. That's a very, very variable amount, and sometimes the meal and the restaurant are so special that there is simply no way of knowing how much to charge until you charge it. It's valuable to the people who choose to dine at the restaurant, and if the restaurant suddenly cut their prices dramatically, they'd actually *lose* many of their regulars who go there because they think the restaurant is special.

How to transition from hourly billing

So, how does all this relate to your hourly rates as a consultant offering some service?

It's highly pertinent, because it shows that the price you charge shouldn't be based on the time it takes you to do your service. You can perform your work much faster than others, but charging at an a similar hourly rate to them (even if it's a bit higher) means you'll get paid less than them.

Value in the Eye of the Beholder

Perhaps you're wondering "how do I get to the value?"

Obviously in a restaurant you can't ask each of the guests: "what is this meal worth to you?" You'd lose all your patrons if they had to go through that process every time they came to eat.

Although, when you think about it, that's *exactly* what they do, unless you have only one item on the menu. They may be judging on price, their appetite, their usual eating habits, their health needs, how tired and hungry they are … all sorts of reasons.

What if you could walk through that decision-making process for big IT contracts? What if you – the consultant – could have the conversation with the end client about what the project was really worth to them? What if you could ask them about the business value of their project, so that instead of charging for your hours of input, you could charge based on the value of the result for their business?

What would that conversation look like?

CHAPTER 5: Let's Talk About Value

Since I've moved myself off hourly pricing – and moved my clients away from it – I've become remarkably detached from worrying about hourly rates or daily rates. In fact, *I even try to talk clients out of using me.*

How counter-intuitive is that?

There's a reason behind this approach.

You see, when you buy something that is anything but a low-cost or impulse purchase, you tend to um and ahh about it. You weigh up the pros and cons, try to put up some objections of why you shouldn't buy this and then, of course, answer those objections.

I'm an IT guy who is very comfortable talking about the technical aspects. I'm not in sales and I would never consider myself good at selling anything.

Now if even this non-salesy tech nerd can understand this, so can you.

When the client raises objections, it's not a sign they're not interested. Of course, it depends on the objection. But if they have written you off right from the start, you won't be having much of a conversation about the objections.

So, why do I try to talk them out of using my services?

Simple. It's my way of controlling and guiding the conversation about objections. Because people usually won't tell you why they didn't choose to use you. So if you have that conversation with them up front, you've got a much better chance of giving them a ready answer to their objections.

"Why would you hire me?"

You never want to make a quick buck. In fact, the most important thing you can do for your client is to demonstrate to them that you're working in *their* best interests. Sounds sales-y, right?

Well, the most effective way of demonstrating your willingness to work as a partner and not a vendor is to understand their business problem. Note that this is understanding it *from a business point of view*. In other words, **don't talk technical!**

In practice, that means you have to identify the pain point. The pain point is what the client *perceives* is costing them money or time or is exposing the business to some risk or missed opportunity.

Note very well: the *perceived* pain point may not be the real problem at all. In fact, you may find yourself telling them: "that's actually not a problem at all. The system is meant to work that way."

Or you could find that what they think is a risk is actually a symptom of some far bigger exposure to the business that they hadn't taken into account.

It's important to find where the pain is that they're feeling, and *what the real cause of it is.*

Did someone say "urgent"?

I know a dry cleaner who told me that some of the oldest items of clothing that hadn't been picked up were the ones marked as urgent. The customer had come in and needed the dry cleaning done ASAP, then for some reason they found that they didn't need it quite so urgently.

I find the same thing often happens when you're working on an IT project. Someone will say "this is urgent", but as a professional, you'll need to understand *why* it's so urgent.

This is very, very important. You want to know the business impact of this "urgent" project.

Now maybe it really *is* urgent. Or perhaps there's a workaround. The point is you really have to drill down to find the heart of the problem.

Getting Beneath the Symptoms

So, when a client contacts me and says "we need this", I'll directly or more indirectly walk them through a series of questions.

- Why do you need it?
- *When* do you need it?
- Why is it urgent?
- What happens if you don't get it by then?

- Is there some workaround, or some way of accelerating a different project to relieve the pressure on this one?

This is very, very important, because it's not in anyone's interest to have you working on a project that isn't going to achieve the client's business goals.

Really, when you drill down to find out why the client's business is dependent on this piece of work, you are stepping back from your technical role and focusing on their business. That already will single you out from other technical people who will jump into a technical solution.

"You Don't Want to Hire Me!

The next part really takes some nerve, because it's risking the whole deal.

Now that you've understood the business goals – at least a little – you can find out what you can do to meet those goals. And then you walk them through the alternatives.

So, you might ask questions like:

- Can't you do this in-house?
- Have you looked online for someone?
- Can't you just do nothing about this risk, but increase your business insurance?

I've even asked clients if they would use my competitors. I admit, I'll generally only do that if I've already had some indication from the client that the competitors didn't answer their questions … usually because those competitors just never returned the client's call.

This line of discussion is a way to get the client to resolve in their own minds all of the objections that are most likely to come up after you've left the building and they've discussed this project with someone else. Instead of that happening, you're able to demonstrate your value (we're not talking price here!). And the way to do that is by showing that you understand the *business* problem that they have identified.

If you think this attempt to answer the client's objections in your presence is sneaky, think of how a doctor works. You go to the doctor with a symptom – say it's chest pains. The doctor will then ask you about the symptoms, do some tests and may discover that the chest pains are to do with something totally unrelated to what you first feared.

The doctor's job is to diagnose, not to let you self-diagnose. And if the doctor generally believes that there is someone else who can treat you better, such as a specialist in a particular field, the doctor would be wrong to hide that from you.

Making the Client Find the Value

Discussion about the business value of a project not only demonstrates your interest in the client's needs. It also forces the client themselves to delve deeply, to find out why this or that pain point is really a problem, and to find out whether what you propose to diagnose – and perhaps ultimately solve – that problem is in the client's best interests.

Can you see how this transition from hourly rates to understanding the client's real problem is good for your client / consultant relationship?

So, when someone asks you what your it will cost to build a bridge across a river, you might not just jump into the technical details:

- What sort of bridge do you want?
- Is it for motor vehicles or just foot traffic?
- What materials do you want it made of?
- When do you want it completed?

In fact, you could find alternatives to a bridge, such as a ferry or swimming lessons.

But really, your job is not just to find out what sort of

bridge they want, or even other means they could use to cross the river. The real value is finding out why they want to go from where they are to the other side of the river in the first place.

There's something even better about this "do-you-really-need-to-hire-me?" approach: the client is the one articulating why you're the person who can help them out of their mess. You haven't just identified the pain and the cause; you've also shown them the path forward, *and* addressed their objections. This is very much in the interests of both you and the client, because you're both on the same page.

CHAPTER 6: The Next Step

The aim of this book was to show you that hourly charging is damaging for your consulting business. In my view, it can undermine the relationship of trust between you and the end client, and that in turn can lead to resentment on the part of the consultant.

I understand that it's not always an easy transition from hourly rates. After all, they're standard across many industries, and there's often a convenience factor which makes it harder for clients to agree to a different model of pricing … especially if there is an agent in between the client and the consultant.

However, I believe that charging per project, especially if it is based on the value to the client, rather than the input of the consultant, is a workable and very fruitful model.

From my experience, clients themselves are very happy when they know there is a fixed budget that they can factor in at the start of the project. A project estimate of hours is not a fixed price. And – on top of fixed pricing – the client is getting value-based pricing, so the return on investment is much more attractive than simply an hourly rate which is seen as an expense item.

There's a good deal more to be said about hourly pricing and how to move away from it. This book really aims to answer *why* you should move away from it.

For more details on *how* to go about removing yourself from hourly based charging, and how to escape the Timesheet Trap, I'd recommend you have a look at the material from Brennan Dunn, who is the creator of Double Your Freelancing Rate and Double Your Freelancing Clients, which are both courses that have helped me and thousands of others to learn how to price their services. (Full disclosure: I am a paying student of Brennan's courses. I do not get any affiliate fees for these links).

Brennan has a lot of free material available on his website, but this article in particular covers – at a very high level – the question:

Should Freelancers Bill By The Hour?

Here is a short article that addresses the same issue. This one is by David Masters. Is This Common Freelancing Mistake Costing You Money?

For me, one of the first people to articulate the idea of *not* billing by the hour was Jonathan Stark. He has an outline of his method of value-based pricing on his website, ExpensiveProblem.com.

Finally, there are two other books which I'd recommend for this topic. One is by Alan Weiss and it's called Value Based Fees: How to Charge – and Get – What You're Worth. I would also recommend the book by Sean D'Souza called The Brain Audit – Why Customers Buy and Don't Buy. It is not directly on hourly-based pricing but it covers a number of very illuminating ideas on how to articulate your value to a potential client.

ABOUT THE AUTHOR

Anthony English works as an Information Technology consultant in Sydney, Australia. He regularly writes for online magazines about his field of expertise – IBM Power Systems.

He is also very active encouraging other consultants from around the world to build their business by charging what they are worth.

Anthony is available for podcasts and interviews. You can contact him via email at anthony@anthonyenglish.com.au

www.ingramcontent.com/pod-product-compliance
Lightning Source LLC
Chambersburg PA
CBHW070405190526
45169CB00003B/1115

* 9 7 8 1 5 3 0 6 9 1 8 7 6 *